Finger My Pages

Carrie Turner

Prologue:

I think experience shapes a person into who they are at each successive stage in their life. These are my experiences. I hope they help you understand me and thus parts of yourself that you may have been afraid to explore before. Purging these words from my head made room for new words and art. Upon asking my friend, Dearest Douglas, to read them and assist me in revising my words into a better flow for you, the reader, I realized I felt naked and exposed. I thought this is how I will feel when "the world" reads it. I decided I needed to continue with this journey, because one can't learn and grow unless they push themselves past their comfort zones. I'm pushing me. I'm pushing you.

Special thanks to:

My husband, Andy Turner, for making sure I eat and shower and go to sleep during times I'm so focused that I sit in one spot not moving. And for his never ending love and support of every endeavor I try.

My friend, editor, proofreader and thought-provoker, Douglas Crabtree, who helped form my thoughts and ramblings from a framework shell to a full-fledged being.

And, last but not least, and certainly the most important. Thank you to every person reading this and to those who have come in and out of my life to shape my experiences to create the following out of those encounters.

Disclaimer/Warnings:

The best way to describe the following writings would be Hugh Hefner's version of Fifty Shades of Grey or Madonna's sex book in words instead of photos. If you can't handle that, don't read this book.

Maybe it's fiction. Maybe it's non-fiction. You decide. In the event the stories contained herein are real, names and revealing locations or details have been changed to protect the guilty.

What's inside my pages...

5. Thoughts from a Tissue

6. My First Memories of Sex

12. All About My Vagina

13. 25 Random Things

15. Three-Way Relationship

17. Butterfly

18. Girls, Girls, Girls

19. Encounters with a Lesbian

21. Moonlight

22. My First Lesbian Fuck

23. My Hair

24. Movie Theater with a Girl I've Never Met Before

25. College Days Away From Home

27. Rain

28. I'm in Love

32. Wintry Escape

33. Why Do You Do This to Me?

34. Evolution of Life Mirrored in Nail Polish

35. Not So Vanilla Anymore

36. Sub Rules and Code of Conduct

38. Task 1

39. Task 2/Task 3

40. Washing Master

41. Yo – Yo

42. Blowjob for Master

43. Gum

44. How I Think About Master Fucking Me

45. Empty Stomach

46. A Strap-On/Spank-Filled Fantasy

48. Get Out of My Head

49. A Playdate Provided by Master

50. Tree Energy

51. The Mistress of the House and Her Slave

52. It's Beauty

53. Pressure: A Dream

54. Slippery When Oiled

56. Nylon, Pink Ball Gag, and Peach Pie: A Photo Shoot Gone Wild

58. Katie Tries for the BIG-O

73. Orgasm

73. Change is Good?

74. I wish I was a butterfly…

76. About The Author

Thoughts from a Tissue

Blow me.
Use me.

Make me wet.

Squeeze me.
Crumple me.

Make me sweaty.

Rub me.
Hold me.

Keep me close.

You need me.

My First Memories of Sex

I remember my first sexual exploration happening when I was about 8 years old. This was when I began my discovery of the body (mine and others'), with all its secret, thrilling, disturbing parts. My Girl Scout troop was holding a sleep over. Although it was indoors, the girls all pitched tents to sleep in, just like we were in the wild under the stars. Two of my girl friends and I shared a tent. We watched movies, ate popcorn, giggled and chattered like girls do. Well, we for some reason, decided to put our hands in each other's pants and touch one another's pussies. One girl whispered that if she put her finger inside then I would get pregnant...so, for ages after that night, I was freaked and afraid I might be pregnant. I don't think she even put her fingers all of the way in me (if it's even comfortably possible to at that age). We never afterwards spoke of doing this with each other. Instead of it bringing us closer together, it came between us, embarrassed us, and pushed us all apart as friends.

My next sexual memory, from about age 10 to 12, is of learning how to masturbate. I'm not sure why...but one day I decided to touch myself WHILE peeing. Now that was nice! So, for a long time I would touch myself whenever I peed, finally figuring out how to cum like that. I also turned myself around on the toilet so I was straddling it, facing the back, and would pee like that (sitting down) pretending I was a guy and touch myself. I was a long time figuring out how I could make it feel good when I wasn't peeing too.

At night in my bunk bed I would masturbate imagining a guy spooning me from the back and feeling him get hard against my back. That felt so comforting and grown up that it turned me on and I started to touch. Sometimes I would do it during the day in my parent's bedroom so I could watch out the window to tell if they were coming in the house. One time my dad walked in the room and I fell off the bed trying to pull my pants up. He asked me what I was doing and I said I dropped something... so embarrassing! On this strange note, I put on my dad's jock strap a couple times because I thought it was some kind of "sex underwear" and it made me feel naughty. Yes, sick, I know. I'm still turned on by jock straps.

I was in 4-H, a youth group that shows animals at the fair, amongst other things. I would go to 4-H camp from age 13-19, and to the fair, and I was always so awkward around guys. I felt like a really dorky nerdy person. Not much happened here, except flirting. One time, late on a Friday or Saturday evening, I made out with a guy in his camper at the fair, sitting on his lap rubbing on him with some other kids there. Fair and camp were always times to wear your hottest clothes, even around the stinky animals, and flirt with boys. No kissing here...just rubbing and groping. Other people I knew had full blown sex and relationships in campers. But, I was a good girl for most of my formative years. Not that I wasn't interested in sex. I thought about it a lot actually. I just didn't want to get pregnant and disappoint my parents. Plus, I was not confident enough to know HOW to get boys to talk to me as more than a friend.

There was a time once in high school I did sneak off with a guy friend. We were in his car in a church parking lot (it's sacrilege you say?) after dark and we were hugging in the front seat and I was laying across him with my back to him. He felt my breasts and I was really turned on, but knew it wasn't a good idea to encourage him further.

I didn't even kiss a guy or girl until I began working at a grocery store. I was 19. At the same time, I started college, going first to the branch for two years, then to the main campus for my last two. So I got a job, my license, and started college all when I was 19. Late blooming was my game.

Talking to people in line at the grocery store was hard for me, at first, because guys would flirt with me, and I was clueless how to respond. I <u>wanted</u> to flirt back, but being inexperienced, didn't really know how. I was a bagger for two days, cashier for two months, and then promoted to the office. The office manager was a giant pervert of a guy... always throwing sexual innuendos. I shot back as good as he gave, because I liked the attention. I found out he had gotten in big trouble before for sexual harassment, but I liked it. Being an office worker and in charge of counting money and telling cashiers what to do, combined with the increased flirting, made me feel powerful. And this is when I started getting really naughty. Now I developed the confidence I'd lacked in high school. So, I started seriously blooming around age 19, from attention. I've found attention makes me and a lot of people bloom. All people want is to be wanted.

The first guy I made out with was Don. I met him in college at the branch campus; and I told him I was a virgin. He said I was hot and so we went to the movies and then parked on the side of a road. I drove so he was in the passenger seat. We started touching each other... no kissing (not sure why not). I moved over and got on top of him. We took off our pants and rubbed ourselves together for a while. My God it felt good! So I accidentally on purpose moved so he slipped inside of me. After a couple moves I felt guilty and told him I couldn't and got off him. He said that was ok. I felt like bad things could happen from having sex. I suppose they can, too, in terms of STDs and unwanted pregnancies. But, I think the biggest reason for not taking things further was because of my parents. I didn't want them to find out or to feel like I had let them down. I didn't have a strict, religious, no-sex-before-marriage upbringing, but we were brought up with clear expectations of what was right and what was wrong. And, according to my mom, sex without love was wrong. Speaking to her later on in life, I don't know if she would have agreed or not that sex can just be recreational, but I think she would have. I'm sure she told me that, because that's what parents do, and she didn't want me to be hurt or get into a bad situation. I get my penchant for worry from my mom.

The next guy... I don't even remember his name now. Let's call him Rob. (You'll find I don't remember most of their names, which is a little sad I suppose.) I met him at the grocery store. He was a customer. He would come in, go through my check out line, and hit on me. He asked me out to the fair and I agreed. At that time I still lived with my parents while I went to college so I had to tell them. They just said okay. He told me he was 30 which wasn't a big age difference as I was almost 20. Turns out he was more like 35 or maybe more. My parents were not happy, but I went out with him a lot and considered him my boyfriend. We met in the grocery store parking lot and he said he needed to get something at his house before we went. I was wary about this, but I'm naive so I got in his truck. At his house, in his kitchen, he said... give me a kiss. I said ok, but didn't move because I had never kissed anyone before and didn't know what to do first. Also, I was nervous. My heart was pounding with excitement and a touch of fear, being in a strange man's house. So, he moved in and kissed me. Open mouth... tongues... fireworks. I got a hot flash and thought oh my God, why have I never done this before? I would have kept kissing and kissing him, but he pulled away. People talk about seeing stars? <u>I saw stars</u>. The kiss I didn't remember very much, and still don't. It's the feeling I remember... the excitement... the way he wanted me... his passion for me. It was intoxicating for sure. Kisses are a heady drug that make you forget the world around you. He asked me if I liked that. Uh, YEAH. So we went to the fair and held hands all through it. I had a boyfriend now, and was holding his hand in public! This meant I was grown up; someone wanted me, so all of the boys before who hadn't approached me would see now that I was desirable. Ever notice how no one wants you until you are with someone else, then they all do? I have read it's been proven that does happen. When we went back to his house, he wanted to watch movies. So, he turned on the TV while I sat on the couch. Then, he didn't waste any time. He stood up in front of me and unzipped his fly and pulled out his cock. He told me to kiss it. So I kissed the head. Then he said open your mouth a little and I did. He pushed his cock in my mouth and basically fucked my mouth. It wasn't hard. It was gentle and my mouth was moist and ready. I was confused knowing I probably shouldn't be doing this, but enjoying it all the same. I could taste his precum but didn't realize he was going to cum so fast. He shot a load of cum in my mouth and I swallowed it. What else could I do with it? I was so naive I didn't have a clue as to my options. He said, "You've never done that before? You did it perfectly like you've had practice." I guess I must just be a natural.

He was my boyfriend for maybe a couple of months. My dad kept telling me that a guy of his age would not keep going out with me without getting something. What my dad didn't know was that he was getting something. We would take his truck out on the back roads, pull over, and I would give him a blow job. It made me feel powerful to be able to make him cum so fast. It still does make me feel powerful and hot and very wanted when I can make a guy cum fast. Like it's uncontrollable and they want me so bad they can't help it. Anyway, one time in his house he wanted to go down on me. I had a big ole hairy bush and he was the first one to tell me it might be good to trim it. So I cut it with scissors. After I started going to college at the main campus in Athens, I thought one day in the dorm shower, what the hell, I'll just shave it all off and be done with it. I learned that the first time itches like hell. And if you wait too long to shave it... then it's like starting all over again with the itch... so I kept shaving it every day. Later on, I Naired my asshole too just for fun and kept doing that too. So, back to my "boyfriend"... he would lick me, but it didn't do anything for me. Naturally, he kept trying to fuck me, but I didn't want to get pregnant, and I think he didn't want to use a condom. I was too inexperienced to ask if he wanted to use one or not, probably how a lot of teenage pregnancies happen. One time I was on top of him and rubbing and I just grabbed it and put it in for a second because I couldn't take it anymore, it being the exquisite torture. So lovely! So thick and filling! I was seriously unfulfilled and whiny when I climbed off of him with a sigh. I think shortly after that my dad made me break up with him. He was a construction worker and my dad said he was not good for my future. Boo, but oh well. Parents do know best sometimes.

It was weird being with guys I worked with because my mom worked at the grocery store too, so all this was really covert. But, this one guy who was, again, about 35 did ask me out, a slim, shy, unaggressive guy who worked in the meat department. I went to his house; and now I was the initiator. I kissed him. Not a good kiss, too dry. Imagine when you feel nauseous and your mouth is dry. That's what it was like. He lived alone and was a lonely person. Somehow we got in the position to fuck from the kissing. I remember it was Christmas time and he had a tree up. Anyway, he was rubbing his pelvis against mine. It was repetitive and soothing. This is one of the few times I actually came from sex. And I came fast. I was such a dork... I said, "Oh my God, thank you". He just said, "You are welcome". And then he didn't even try to cum, which was good, because we were having unprotected sex. Looking back now, I don't think he was even inside of me. Then he got off me and asked me if I wanted a drink or to hang out, but I was really only there for one reason. So, I left and went home. He asked me out again, but I didn't really like him, so I declined. I think the kissing turned me off and knowing he was another type that would not be good for my future. The age difference was too large.

Another guy I worked with was a cashier and kind of a "player". Not having good self-confidence, I didn't think he would be interested in me. But one time I asked him out or he asked me. Somehow we just asked each other. I went to his grandma's house with him and we made out on her bed. No sex. I think he wasn't sure if I would, nor was I sure if he wanted to. Communication is always key in any relationship and getting what you want!

One time there was another cashier who walked me to my car after dark. He got in my passenger side. We were talking and he asked me if I wanted to see his cock. I was like...um sure? So he got it out and started touching it. I didn't really like him. He asked me to touch it and so I did. And then he said I want to cum. I said get out. He said not until I cum. So he wanked himself until he came in my car and made me watch. A couple years later he came to the main campus with a friend of mine and made another friend of mine do the same thing. She was very uncomfortable about it. She kind of wanted to watch him and touch it, but at the same time felt guilty as she was in a relationship. That guilt will get you every time! Later on this particular guy was fired for stealing more than $5,000 over time out of the register while he was a cashier.

Then I went out with another guy from the meat department. Yes, a second from the meat department. I DO like meat though. He was a pot smoking poor white trash kid who always played video games. Most of the time when we were at his house he would play video games. I wanted him to fuck me... so this didn't last long. He was a fumbler, meaning the sex was really awkward. He was more interested in his video games than sex. Later on I realized he wanted one of my friends who was a lesbian; and I was jealous. Interesting that I was jealous considering she only liked girls and wouldn't have wanted him anyway. But, it's still hurtful to not feel wanted by the one you choose to be in a relationship with.

I dated a freaky guy that liked Insane Clown Posse and was going to pierce his own body in various places. Anyway, I told him if he went down on me...I'd do the same. He started kissing me and the kissing was too much tongue down my throat. It was wet and sloppy, aggressive, which I'm a fan of, but his lips didn't seem to stay on my lips only. They were covering my face, like a dog, in sloppy kisses. I was thinking this is not good, but we got in the back seat of my car and I took off my pants and he started licking and kissing my pussy. He had a goatee. I'm not sure if it was the goatee or the right pressure or he kept doing the same thing over and over but I actually came... first and only time from oral. I was in such a happy daze that I said, "I'm too tired, I'll do you another time." But I never did.

All About My Vagina

My vagina looks like an albino bat.

My vagina smells just like sin and spice and everything nice.

I call my vagina a pleasure pocket... just kidding. I never call it that, but I should.

I think my vagina is great because it matches all my birthday suit outfits!

A special treat for my vagina is beggin' strips.

My vagina likes loose panties.

If my vagina could talk it would sound like mrrrroooowwwwrrrr (giant kitty noise).

25 Random Things

1. I can't swim.
2. I hate receiving cut flowers. They just die.
3. All of the knick knacks I buy and my mom gave me drive me crazy, but I don't know how to get rid of them. (Because some I do like... but I like the clean look better.)
4. I'm a Gemini... so I have two sides... and I waffle back and forth a lot. (See #3 for an example)
5. I'm lactose intolerant... no cheese, no milk, no chocolate. I'm also gluten free. I'm totally fine with it. It's the other people that feel sorry for me.
6. Every time I get dressed for work I feel like I'm still a kid playing dress up going off to work in the big real world.
7. I wanted to be an archeologist when I was growing up and still would like that.
8. My plan in high school was to be a fashion designer and live in New York. I still would like that also.
9. I often eat cookies for dinner... and break... and lunch.
10. I want a maid and a pool boy (and a pool to go with it even though I can't swim)... and a midget.
11. Nothing you say sexually will shock me. Try me. I've heard or read it all (and so will you by the end of this book).
12. I have a very dirty mind and think about sex more times a day than a guy.
13. I didn't get my driver's license until I was 19 because I was afraid of car accidents. I ended up being in one with a friend driving and now I get motion sickness.
14. I had boxes and boxes of trophies (close to 70) in the basement from when I showed goats, chickens, geese, ducks, and rabbits in 4-H at the fair (age 8-19). I donated them all to the fair so they could refurbish them and use them again.
15. My favorite color is fuchsia/magenta. I know they are different colors. But I always think of them as interchangeable.
16. Watching my parents age scares me.
17. I hate sad movies, sad books, and anything in general that is aimed at making me cry.
18. I always make Andy turn the channel or mute the TV if someone on it is barfing.

19. So far, if I could take back anything in my life... I wouldn't.
20. Cleaning is over rated. So I usually don't do it.
21. I get excited when I have a new message in my Facebook inbox. Such potential.
22. I have a superstition that once I see an e-mail is a chain letter, if I haven't read all the way to the end, I don't have to send it on to avoid the bad luck.
23. I'd really like to have purple (or some other crazy color) hair as my permanent hair color.
24. I think I'm a genius, but haven't taken the test. I guess as long as I don't take it... I can keep thinking that.
25. I love that freshly crapped feeling.

Three-way Relationship

In my next relationship I was part of a three way. I met the girl first. We had a class together. She was high energy, a bubbling burst of smiles, cheer, happiness, and beauty. I'd really not considered being in a relationship with women too much, but I liked her as a person. And that for me is always the most important factor in attraction. Gender doesn't matter so much as a person's brain and personality. She was fun and included me and made me feel cool like no one else did. Her boyfriend was in a local band...and SUPER hot. He had blond hair. I usually prefer dark hair on men and women. She would invite me to their gigs. We'd flirt and act crazy to make the boys look at us... typical girls-going-out behavior. I think her boyfriend wanted to fuck me and didn't know how to make that happen. Together they worked it out that they wanted to add me to their relationship. The stipulation was that I couldn't do anything with either of them if the other wasn't present. Eventually....that caused the break up...

We would, all three, go to the movies, and sit in the back row together. We would hold hands in the lobby and in the theatre itself. Why should we care if people looked at us? In fact, I'd say I liked the attention. Attention whore, probably so. She worked at a book store in the mall and I would meet her when she didn't have customers there. We would go in the back room and make out. He would practice in the sound-proof music room at the college, and I would go in with him and make out. The make out sessions were very heavy. I don't remember actual sex happening, but I'm sure she wouldn't have been happy to know that was going on. I found them both attractive and wasn't trying to pit one against the other. I suppose I just didn't understand (since it wasn't my relationship that started it all) why I couldn't hang out with them independently of each other. And, not understanding, it didn't seem like a rule that should apply to me. I don't think they told each other about these times when I was with them separately.

Once we were at a party and she and I got drafted for a beer run. It was late at night and we were holding hands. The old guys at the grocery store kept watching us. I had to pee so I went to the bathroom there. It was big enough for one, but she came in too. I peed and wiped and stood up. Before I could pull up my pants she was licking me. I leaned against the wall because it felt so good. The entire night with her was foreplay, so I felt ripe and full and wanton. She didn't lick very long. I loved what she did and wanted her to keep going. It was really one of my first interactions with a woman orally, so that made it feel more naughty and interesting also. When she stopped I pulled up my pants and we went out, bought the beer, and went back to the gig like nothing had happened… giggling and holding hands.

I was more their little sex toy than anything else. They would both play with my breasts and Lexie coined the phrase "cupcake titties" to describe my adorable little boobs. Hers were bigger than mine. She was so beautiful! They were a hot alternative looking couple with a basket full of sex toys. She would fuck me with a vibrator, and then fuck herself while he fucked me for real. I never actually licked her pussy. I'm not sure if she didn't care if I did or it just didn't line up. I was a bit naïve at that time I guess, so maybe she did want me to, but she never asked or put her pussy in my face... so I'm not sure. I did touch her pussy, and I hugged her and stroked her and touched her all over. She seemed to enjoy watching his cock go in and out of me. I'll agree that repetition of movement is mesmerizing.

Once driving back to my parents I got pulled over by the cops trying to get home, since I was out past curfew. Yes I was 19+ and had a curfew, but you know the deal. "If you live at home, you live by our rules." I was going 65 in a 55 and got a ticket. I just paid it and never told them.

My beautiful alternative couple ended up splitting up, I think, because they were both jealous of the other being with me. And so that relationship ended.

Years later I spoke to her. He was a bit of a womanizer she told me, and in spite of them having an open relationship, it was too much. Personally, I do think open relationships can work with the right combination of people and communication. But, that combination is rare.

Butterfly

Flit ~ float ~ fly
Away

Here ~ there ~ everywhere
Try this ~ try that

Dreams transforming into reality.

Wings stretching and flexing,
soaring the skyline,
higher and higher.

Drifting down to the
garden of life below.

Consuming sweet nectar,
brightens wing color.

Recharged ~ revitalized ~ alive
for the moment.

Searching for the next
flower to land upon.

The flight is over.
Or is it?

Where is the next flower?
Why are they so hard to find?

I'm a butterfly.
I'm a bird.
I'm a bee.
I'm whatever I want to be!

Girls, Girls, Girls

This brings me to my lesbian phase. My best friend from grade school is a lesbian. Some people in school thought the same of me due to a mistake that ended up shaping many of my formative years. In 6th grade, in the locker room after gym, I smacked a popular girl on the ass. I honestly did not think this weird because at home we did it all of the time joking around. There it meant nothing... here, apparently, it made me gay. I was traumatized and afraid to touch anyone from that point forward for fear of being called more names or labeled an outcast. To this day, I still shy from people. I love hugs and I want hugs and to overcome this I force myself to hug people. Interestingly, that popular girl from school now actually IS a lesbian (although she wouldn't have known that then). Being so visible, and going through that in that time and place, I'm sure she was projecting onto me.

In high school, I went to several parties and was friends with a group of lesbians. A couple of them worked at my grocery store. That's how we met. All of them I ended up kissing at one party or another. I loved and still do love to kiss girls. It's kind of forbidden... not supposed to be a girl and kiss the girls... so makes it feel hotter. One girl I was in lust with. She would tease me mercilessly. At the grocery store's Christmas party, with my parents and all our co-workers around, she and a friend of hers took me into the bathroom with them. Her friend watched the door and she led me into a stall. This made me think they had an agenda. We looked at each other and just started kissing like crazy. To this day... still the hottest fucking kiss I ever had. It was wild and aggressive and ungirl-like. Most women probably like other women because they are soft and girly. I like them more masculine. I like them to come after me like a guy, yet be a girl. She said that I was more forward than she thought I would be. Had she wanted me I'd be a lesbian right now. But she was a girl player, and I just another conquest. She was really butch looking, yet slender... and hot. If she had tried, she would have been a hot "regular" girl... but the butch look was working for her.

After that kiss, we went out on the dance floor and slow danced with my parents watching. I was too into her to notice the disapproving looks from them. Just being near her gave me brain fog, so I didn't think about what I should and shouldn't be doing in a crowded room with my parents around.

Encounters with a Lesbian

I knew she was gay... "dyke-level" gay. Short with D-cup boobs, super tomboyish, her short hair in a Mohawk and lots of piercings – the complete opposite of me. One day, I'd expressed an interest to go with her and her friends to a gay bar they frequented in the city. She remembered that, and asked me if I wanted to come hang out and drink in her dorm room some time with the gang. I said I would love to hang out. So, then we started talking more and more. Talking led to flirting...

One day, she sat down by my desk and began picking magnets off of it. She held one out to me and I took it, but took it really slowly, our hands touching the whole time. Three times she did that. The last time, though I didn't know it, there was nothing in her hand. So, I just took her hand and locked fingers. She scooted back to her desk pretty fast after that. She got embarrassed easily, and so did I. She messaged me and told me I had soft hands. I was thinking the same about her. That moment when we locked fingers felt like an electric shock.

She kept telling me to meet her in the last stall in the bathroom at school. I kept refusing, but now finally, I agreed. That shocked her! I walked into the bathroom, and grabbed the handle of the last stall and pulled. Someone was in there taking a shit! No one's ever in there! So, we went to separate stalls and – duh! – weren't thinking, so we didn't even flush or anything to make it seem real. We walked out and across the hall into an empty classroom and sat down. We sat across from each other in swivel chairs, sitting kind of scissored so our legs touched. We talked about how embarrassing that was in the bathroom. Finally I said, "Time's up". So she stood up and on her way out, paused by my chair. She gave my hair a slow stroke down its length then, all of a sudden, jerked my head back. Her mouth was drawing close to mine. I breathed in and said, "Oh god".... and knew she was going to kiss me. And she did. And I licked her lip piercing. And her soft hand held mine, which was between my legs. And, then we thought we heard someone coming and booked it back to our seats. We both had bright red faces I'm sure. That moment was an ice breaker. It was clear we both wanted more.

I told her I would take her out on a date... to lunch. We met in the back of the parking lot of the restaurant. Thinking about her made me nervous, and excited, and not really hungry... for food. I asked her if she wanted to give me a tour of her car. She said, "Shit yeah". So she pulled up and I got in the passenger seat. We talked a bit and she was very nervous. "Move over and sit on my lap", I said. She claimed there was no room, but moved her own seat back. So I crawled across and got on her lap. She grabbed my ass/hips to help move me. Then I leaned down and kissed her. We kissed and rubbed and licked for a while, the windows going up and down because my legs kept pushing buttons. I guided her hand up and put it on my bare boob under my shirt, unbuckled her belt, and slid my hand down her pants. I wasn't sure what to do at first, but I just touched around and found her soft slit, and started stroking with my finger. I realized how wet INSIDE she was, and the more I touched the wetter she got. She was soaking her boxer briefs. (Yes, she wore boxer briefs, like a guy.) She kept asking me to go back to her room with her. I was reluctant. But, I compromised and we moved to the back seat. I was on top. I sucked her neck, collarbone and nipples. I told her, "Put your hand down your pants and touch yourself." Since I wasn't sure what to do to make her happy, I wanted to see where she touched, so I pulled her pants away from her to watch. That turned her on! Then I asked if I could lick her and she grabbed my hair and pushed my mouth onto her, and I licked her with just my tongue. I wanted to put all of my mouth on her, but her pants and the car impeded me. It was my first time licking a girl's clit. It was like taking her all the way into me – the little mauve-painted toes wriggling as they slip past my teeth – and then having her melt over my tongue. Then she pushed her sopping fingers into my mouth and made me suck off her slime. I licked and sucked her fingers for a long time, loving the raunchy taste and smell of her, so tangy-sweet and syrupy. In a trance she watched me do it. The whole car must have smelled like bitch-in-heat. Why dogs didn't rush up and hump the tires, I'll never know.

She asked me back to her dorm, I agreed. We went to her room. She locked the door and threw me on the bed and got on top. She put her leg between mine and grabbed my hips and rubbed me, crotch to leg. I was humping her like you'd dry hump a guy. Her aggression really turned me on. I was trying not to be loud. She said, "Shhhhh"! I said, "You have to stop doing that if you don't want me to be loud!" I was on the last day of my period too, so I was trying to keep my pants on. I told her that, but she pushed her fingers inside me and finger fucked me. My leg started shaking. Neither of us came, but we weren't trying to. She had to strip off her boxer briefs because all her juices had soaked them through. I shared with her my trick (which you might like too) of always wearing a pantiliner. Then when I get wet, it is absorbed and is not so uncomfortable. Just peel it off and you have the underwear as a backup.

Moonlight

M usic fills the room.
O ak trees sway in the wind.
O wls hoot
N ight time messages.
L ace covers windows
I n country cottages.
G uardian angels
H over above.
T omorrow the sun will shine.

My First Lesbian Fuck

She walked in and I was polite enough to give her a brief tour. But once that was done, I was ready to rumble and I grabbed her hand and pulled her into my room. I put on a Maxwell CD. We lay down and cuddled for a bit. Then I slid on top of her and kissed her 'til she let out this breathy moan. That was like a firecracker. I moaned myself and we both went crazy. We kissed. We bit gently. The bitch wore a bra and I told her not to. So I grabbed her shirt and pulled it and her bra off over her head. Because she didn't arrive as I'd asked, I did it kind of rough, as punishment, so her breasts got pulled up too, and then plopped back down and quivered a bit. Big, soft, pillowy breasts, I liked to touch them. I sucked on her nipples. I sucked from under her and lying on top. She broke away, pulled off my shirt, and did the same to me. The kissing ramped up hotter, faster, wilder and I finagled my hand down her pants.

Once I touch her it's a flood. I pull her pants and underwear off. She's embarrassed to be naked alone, so she grabs hold of my pants and thong and peels me like a grape. We rub on each other naked, touching each other's pussies. Her skin is velvety soft against mine. I go down between her legs and kiss all over her mound and inside her thighs. She shaves her pussy slick as I do. I smell her, inhaling her scent, and flick my tongue lightly on her clit. Her hands are in my hair trying to get me to do it harder without pushing my face onto her. I press her clit harder with my tongue and make her moan again really loudly. I am so turned on, my pussy literally dripping all over the sheet between my legs. I tease and lick and torture her a while, sliding a finger inside. Not to make her cum… just playing with her, exploring her, seeing how she responds. I pull away and move up her body, kissing her all over. She kind of wrestles with me and ends by flipping me over and kissing all down my stomach. She reaches my clit and kisses it… soft and gentle at first, and I think – ugh, this is how a guy would do it, and I <u>hate</u> how guys do it. But, then she puts a pillow under my ass and gets all wolf-bitch on me, licking harder and harder. She pushes her fingers inside and finger fucks me. It feels so good, so intense. But, I do <u>not</u> want to cum. I want <u>her</u> to cum. Ten minutes more she'll have my cum dripping down her wrist. She keeps moving her mouth away and wiping her face on the inside of my thighs. So funny and cute! (I think I'm too sloppy to make friction, so she's trying to get rid of some.

Then I managed to get back on top. I worked a couple fingers in and fucked her, using my mouth and tongue on her for a long time. She gasped out that she's going to cum. And I knew she was too, but she couldn't go over the top. So, I did what I do with me, pulled back a bit and built her back up. She pushed my face away and rubbed her clit fast and hard with my fingers still in her. Juices were all over my face and dripping from my mouth. There was a string of slime from my mouth to her pussy. She was filled with juice like a sweet watermelon. She told me to fuck her harder. And she came on my fingers. Then I kissed her belly and we wrapped ourselves around each other and lay still for a while covered in the smell of pussy.

My Hair

Sunlit honey maple...
bronze colored prisms.

Shifting softness
warming my face.

Coconut scented
dark amber strands
caress like smooth fingers.

Tucked... untucked...
waves escaping to
play in the wind.

Golden threads
dragging through lip gloss...
leaving wet kisses
on my cheek.

Movie Theater with a Girl I've Never Met Before

We all went straight for the last row and everyone was in line for a seat in front of me. So, I just sat down on the end of everyone next to Alicia. We were really early. She and I went to get pop and chips. After the movie started, Alicia was jittery and shifting in her seat a lot. She had her hand down under her ass. The back of her wrist was against my thigh. I could tell she wanted me to grab her hand, but I was waiting. I wanted to grasp the premise of the movie before I got too distracted. I got cold and pulled out my blanket and put it over me and my hand went down beside my thigh again. She grabbed it under the blanket, fingers rubbing fingers... rubbing wrists... nails scratching. It felt comforting to hold someone's hand, but I wasn't thinking I wanted her now. It was just nice to be in the movies close to someone.

Then she started moving her pinky fingers against my thighs and moving her hands more and more between my legs. I had on tight pale gray denim shorts down to my knees and a brown v-neck t-shirt. I knew what she wanted. I kept telling her to be good and put her hand back in mine to hold her hand. But she kept going back between my legs over and over. I had a pantiliner on... and she was rubbing my crotch. I could feel it even through that. I was being very relaxed, but the more she rubbed, the more I opened my legs and got wetter. Still I tried to get her to be good and moved her hand away. She moved her hand up under my shirt and touched my stomach and under the waistband of the shorts. I thought oh no, I have this pantiliner on. So, I continued to move her hands away and hold them. She was very insistent. She tried to unbutton my shorts with one hand and I wouldn't help her.

Finally, she worked her hand down my shorts with them still buttoned. I didn't want her fingers pinching my lips because the shorts were so tight (plus I thought what the hell) so I unbuttoned the shorts and unzipped them. She rubbed my clit for a while in a circle, got her fingers wet, and rubbed my clit in and out kind of bouncing my clit against her fingers. She was squirmy and wiggly in her seat and so was I. It was hard to be quiet and act like nothing was happening so the entire movie theater didn't know. I had my eyes closed for a while and I thought if she keeps doing this I will cum and I don't want to here with her with all of these people. But, I also felt like she had been doing it a while and probably wanted me to cum soon and I wasn't close enough. A couple times I tried to get her to understand I was trying to pull her arm out of my pants, but she kept going. She maybe knew I was getting to the point of not caring and wanting her to make me cum and so she didn't want to stop either.

I pulled her hand out and she wiped her fingers across my stomach and I grabbed her hand and wiped her hand on my pants and shirt, so she wouldn't smell too much like pussy. Then we went back to holding hands. She tried again later to get her hand down my pants.

College Days Away From Home

When I went away to college for my last two years to finish my degree I was not used to all that freedom. So, like many, I went a little crazy. I got drunk for the first time. I had sex with people whose names I didn't even know. I stayed up all night. I got kicked out of a bar. I skipped classes. I ate pizza, ramen, and caffeine-free Mountain Dew. I also suffered a weed-induced paranoia and then never smoked it again.

Boys and parties were everywhere. I don't remember the exact order of most of these things, so I'll just ramble on. I remember being at a party in a dorm and that's where I had a buttery nipple for the first time. A very young guy was there who said "I'm still a virgin, but I don't want to be." So I said "Ok... let's do it". We went in his room and he got on top of me and then passed out. Ha.

My roommate had a boyfriend and she would have sex with him in her bed right next to me under the covers. I'm pretty sure I did the same. We just didn't care. There was nowhere else to have sex if we were both in the room, as it was basically a one bedroom room. So we kind of agreed to just do our thing and ignore each other.

One time I took this guy home from the grocery store and his girlfriend too. He looked like Marilyn Manson. She was thin and petite and pale. She just got her boobs pierced and the Marilyn Manson dude made her show them to me. She pulled up her shirt and her boobs were so little. He fondled them in my car in front of me for a long time. She acted a little uncomfortable and didn't look at either of us.

At another party I got to see fake boobs for the first time up close. I've seen fake boobs only twice in my life. This girl was all prissy though and wouldn't let me touch them. She acted like I was gay when I asked. All I wanted was to know how they felt. She was pretty hot... the perfect sorority girl. The second time I saw fake boobs was more recently. Not long ago my hairdresser, who is the exact same size as me, got a boob job. She let me see them and touch them. They are kind of hard. Because she is thin, you can see a ripply line on the sides of her breasts where the seam of the implant shows through.

One cashier at the grocery store never talked to me. Then he found out I was bisexual – wham! – he was all over me. That label is actually inaccurate in my case. "Pansexual" might be the better term, although many don't know what that means. In the back room he would touch me and tell me I was hot. But, I really think he just wanted to do me and another girl at the same time.

After I got off work at 10 or 11, I would stay and talk to the night stock guys, who were bored and always horny. It was fun flirting with them. I never did any of them, but I saw a couple of their cocks. I didn't really ask. They just were like come back here and look at this. Who am I to say no to free cock education?

I made out with one guy, but I liked his girl friend more (they weren't exclusive), so I was using him in a way. When I asked her, she was offended. She's like "I'm not gay!" I would be flattered if a girl came on to me, even if I wasn't into her. She was kind of young, 18 I think, so maybe she just wasn't used to that yet.

Heath: tall, blond, dark glasses, worked as a bagger. I always thought he was cute. So I invited him to come to my dorm room. This was during the winter break. We had sex... missionary style... on my dorm bed. It wasn't that good... not much kissing... no cuddling... just over and done. Apparently I wasn't done with my period when I thought I was. So there was some brownish old blood fluid on the bed and on his dick. He freaked out. I said it was okay. But he looked traumatized, jumped into his clothes, and got out of there fast after the sex was over.

Daniel was short, half black (I don't mean that as in from the waist down), and worked in the office. He was in love with me. He sent me cards and wanted me to be his girlfriend. The problem was he was really, really short and I didn't think he was cute enough to make up for the lack of height. Sure, he was nice, but not really a frantic sexual connection. And he was so innocent... a virgin. We would hang out and do things a lot though (non sexual things... just as friends). One time, it turned sexual. He was lying on my bed facing out and I got on the bed in front of him... my ass to his front. I grabbed for his hand and put it on my boob. He immediately got a hard on and rubbed/squeezed my boob while I wiggled my butt in his crotch. He was dry humping me for a while. I'm not sure what happened, but I just stopped teasing him and that was that. In general, I tried not to lead him on because I didn't want to hurt him. He was too innocent. I wanted someone dirty and nasty.

Rain

Can you make it rain down on me?

My downpour, my sweet, is copiously divine.
I'll give to you, my sweet, all the wetness
that is mine.

Slow movements,
Soft skin,
Loving done right is never a sin.

My pace is that of a race in decline,
as I merge your flesh into mine.
If this is sin, then a sinner am I,
because love done this way surpasses time.

Can you make it rain down on me?

Yes, simply put,
I'll be Poseidon in the clouds.
I'll pour from my heavens,
into your garden,
a river of heated rain.

I'm grateful for this gloom,
this weather before the blooms.
Stay in with me and build it up.

This darkness is like a gradient shade,
a thankful tint,
to enhance the glow around you.
I'll lock this door,
from the inside, keeping all that's good with us.

Because, I want your rain all over me.

Because, I want your rain all over me.

-- A Collaboration

I'm In Love

I was working at the grocery store when I saw this hot guy always coming in with his mom. He had dark hair and a look to him like he would know what to do to me sexually. He was nice and pleasant to me, and I really just wanted to fuck him. So, the next time his mom came through my line, I gave her the phone number to my dorm and said, "Your son is hot... can you please have him call me?" in my sweetest voice. She had been coming through my line for a while and had gotten to like me. He was hot, she agreed, and said she would give it to him. She did and he called. I remember I had laryngitis when he called… not off to a good start.

We talked on the phone a couple of times and then I drove out to his house to pick him up for a "date". The date consisted of sitting in my car and talking, as he had no money to take me out. He was broke and lived with his parents, who grew and smoked pot. His dad worked in the coal mines. His mom didn't work. He had an older and a younger brother. The younger brother was hot and also wanted me. He was super nice to me and had I said yes he would have gone behind his brother's back, fucked me, and tried to steal me from him. The older brother was cute enough, but mentally imbalanced.

So, on our first date... we talked and then started making out. We were parked in this little spot off the back road that leads to his parent's house. He was in the passenger seat, I in the driver's. I remember the knobs being all annoying in my side while we were making out. He pulled me across so I was sitting on his lap. I think I probably gave him head. I loved the noises he made, like I was the sex goddess he had been looking for his whole life and I made him feel like he was in ecstasy. And he tasted so good. I just couldn't get enough of him. It was close to 3 in the morning when I dropped him off at his house and went back to my dorm. I only did that because I had class at 8 a.m.

He was the reason I got on the pill. I went to Planned Parenthood, started my regimen, waited a month, and then I could have sex without condoms. Even after I was on the pill he would never cum in me. I think that was both of our preference. But I really liked it better the way he came anyway. He would pull it out every time and spray it on me somewhere. Or grab my hair and push his cock in my mouth and cum. My old car still sports cum stains in the back seat from him pulling out and spraying everywhere.

One time we were outside standing beside my car. He had me bent over touching my toes and he was fucking me from behind. My head was kind of banging against the side of my car. We heard his dad pulling up and parking across the creek. I don't think he could see us, but while he was fucking me he yelled, "Hi dad"! Good thing his dad just yelled "hi" back and didn't come over to talk.

Another time I was sleeping with him on the couch and we had been doing the silent wiggle and fuck thing. He was behind me and we were both spooning and facing out. His mom thought we just woke up and were chilling. She couldn't tell we were fucking. We had a blanket over us. So she came in and started watching television flipping through channels and talking to us. He maintained the conversation while I was going crazy trying to be quiet and act normal. He buried his head in my neck and pulled out and came all over the inside of my thighs.

His younger brother always told us not to fuck in his bed. But his bedroom was the only private one as my boyfriend shared a bedroom with the older brother. So we would tell his brother we were going upstairs to play games, but we would fuck in his bed quietly.

I don't think we meant any disrespect to his brother by doing this, but I remember I was straddling one of their kitchen chairs backwards and he sat down on it behind me. He was pushing my front against the back of the chair and rubbing his cock on my ass through his jeans and whispering in my ear. I said stop teasing me. I can't take it. He just kept doing it. So I said we need to fuck right now. You better find somewhere. So that's how we ended up in his brother's room.

One time he was having a party in his house. A bunch of people were there and we were in the midst of them making out. I was on his lap straddling him on the couch and he took out his cock and I sucked him in front of people. It seemed like no one was really watching or caring. I pulled off after a while and was going to try something different because I thought it was taking him a long time, but right when I pulled off he grabbed me and pushed me back down and came in my mouth down my throat. I wasn't expecting that.

Somehow I managed to get him and his two brothers to sit side by side on their couch and all take out their dicks and make them hard so I could compare. My boyfriend's was the best. His younger brother was taller and thinner; and, therefore, his dick was longer and skinnier.

I dated him while I lived in the dorm, so I did him in my bed while my roommate was doing her boyfriend right next to us. And I also dated him when my roommate and I moved out and lived in a house too. He and his younger brother came to visit once and we were all hanging out in my room. I was lying in my bed on my side and he was lying behind me. His brother, in a bean bag across from us on the floor, was drawing on a shoebox or something with a magic marker, and we were all talking. My boyfriend lifted up my skirt from the back and pulled down my panties and was rubbing his cock between my thighs. It was driving me crazy. I don't think his brother even knew what we were doing. Abruptly, my boyfriend got up and went to the bathroom. I later found out he couldn't take it anymore and jerked off into the toilet.

He was frustrated that I couldn't cum just from sex and I didn't really use a vibrator nor have any sex toys then to help me out. I came with him one time in the backseat of my car. He was fucking me and it just felt really good and I was like I need something else. It feels so good. Help me. I was whining and pleading, almost like I was in agony. So he just randomly pushed his finger in my ass and I came immediately. Even though it only happened once, it made me feel a better connection to him and like there was hope for me yet.

We fucked anywhere and everywhere as much as we could. I was insatiable for him. The more we had sex, the more I wanted it. I loved fucking him and he was the first person to tell me he loved me. I was a commitment-phobe at the time and started crying. He said it's okay... we can love each other. So, I trusted him that it was okay and just let myself love him.

We fucked in the back seat of my car most of the time because we could be louder. We fucked when I had a cold and was all snotty. We fucked all the time. I loved it. So, I was very surprised when I came back from my parent's house for Thanksgiving break and found out he had cheated on me with a fat whore. He even said I was the "best lay" he's ever had. If that's the case why would he leave me for her? Before moving back here to Ohio, he was a tow truck driver in California and fucked over 50 girls. He made his own crystal meth there and would stay up days on end. In the long run he would not have been good for me, so it worked out. But I was so sad, heartbroken. I had never broken up with someone I loved before and I cried for days. When I went home over Christmas break I was a wreck. My parents were worried about me. I could only eat Rice Chex cereal. I couldn't or wouldn't eat anything else.

I dated him for 8 months.

Wintry Escape

I'm digging a hole
for me to hide.
It's cold in the snow
but I don't mind.

I'm going to visit.
I got a plan.
I strip off my clothes
and tie my hair in a band.

The shivering starts
and my teeth are chattering.
Crystal snowflakes are falling
onto moist eyelashes.

Everything looks blue
and my skin does too.

My nerves are prickly
and I have a stabbing feeling.
I'm still alive
but I'm barely breathing.

I'm hearing voices.
I'm almost there...

Why Do You Do This To Me?

I'm a teeny tiny piece of trash.
Why don't you want me anymore?
You use me and throw me out your window.
It makes me sad.
It's cold out here.
I'm all alone.
And, now it's snowing! :(

The cars are speeding past.
One of them hit me.
I'm getting shredded and starting to fall apart.
I'm embarrassed everyone has to look at me.

I just want to be frolicking with my friends in a landfill.
I'm sorry I ruin the beauty of your landscapes.

But, it's your own fault.

Evolution of Life Mirrored in Nail Polish

Slowly smooth over curves.
Brush moving in and out.
Immersion... disbursement.

Natural, flesh-tone, transforms to
brilliant tint hugging the hard shell.

Color outside the edges.
Professional. Special. Beautiful. Done.

Nothing lasts forever.
Gradually... lighter, duller, fading away.
Cracking, peeling, chipping.

Only a small piece of the
former luster showing.

Is it time for a new transformation?

Wipe it away. Start over. Clean slate.

Go undercover again or be yourself?
Camouflage or breathe and be free?

Not So Vanilla Anymore

I am not here to educate you about the BDSM lifestyle. To learn more about it, certainly you must do your research. I did at one time stumble into a role as a submissive. I loved my Master. I was enthralled with him. The scenarios and role play were a complete mind fuck. It's so freeing to be a submissive and not have to worry about anything. Decisions are taken away from you. I trusted my Master to make the best decisions for me. It is from him that I learned how to be a Mistress. Because, once you know how to be a good submissive, you know how to play the opposite role as well. And, I was a really good submissive.

Some of the writings that follow stem from that time and state of mind.

Sub Rules and Code of Conduct

1. You are a sub. Submissives have both a mind and a will of their own. They are empowered sexually by a relationship like this and are not degraded or berated as a slave would be. Do not refer to yourself as my slave. You are my sub.
2. You must earn everything. You will earn how I address you (nickname if you will) when you please me. You will earn how I address you when you displease me. Until then you are generically my sub. You will earn rewards. You will earn punishments. You will earn the right to ask me questions.
3. I am to be addressed as Mistress Butterfly. You may abbreviate "Yes Mistress" as "ym" and "No Mistress" as "nm". "Butterfly" may also be abbreviated as "BF".
4. You will not address me as Mistress Butterfly in public, nor will you indicate in any manner in a public area that you belong to me.
5. This situation may be terminated at any time by either of us without question.
6. Keep in mind I do not belong to you. You belong to me. So, I will do what and who I want.
7. You have a real life. This is merely entertainment and should not interfere with your real life, nor any occupations or personal relationships pertaining to it.
8. I will give you tasks with deadlines. You must instantly confirm receipt of each task and ask any questions you may have at that time. This will be your one opportunity to ask pertinent questions, after which you must then complete the task at hand to the best of your ability. I will NOT tolerate half-assedness. I expect full cooperation, full compliance, and rigorous attention to detail. Details are important and if not done correctly, you will displease me and, as a consequence, be punished. I do not want to be disappointed by you. Take your allotted time and do it right! I shall require of you nothing which I have not done myself, or would be willing to do myself.
9. E-mail me your schedule of availability once a week after you know your work schedule. Convert it to Eastern Standard Time (USA East Coast).

10. I am a busy person. I understand you want an active owner; however, I can only give so much. You will need to learn patience.

Read the above twice. I will now address your questions, concerns, or anything you feel I should know before we begin. If you have no such questions or concerns, confirm receipt of this and indicate your full compliance (Yes Mistress).

Task 1

Not all of your assignments will be sexual/pictures/videos, etc. This first one, however, will be. There's a reason for everything, and I appreciate and value your trust in me. Know that anything sent to me will be read/viewed <u>by me only</u> and will be deleted promptly when/if our time is up, or at once upon your request. When I give you assignments that include pics/vids I do NOT want something that you have sent someone else. These must be created specifically for me and with me in mind. They also must be e-mailed to me.

You will provide 2 sets of pictures labeled accordingly.

The first set of pictures should contain 20 pictures of yourself that you have taken for someone else or with someone else in mind.... those already in your private collection of pictures.... perhaps your 20 favorite.... it is up to you. After this... I do not expect to see older pics of you.... so you might want to send me special ones that you want me to see.

The second set of pictures should contain 20 "parts of you". I want the pics to be clear, neither blurry, nor poorly done. They may be nude or not...erotic or not. They must simply show "you" to me in picture form. One pic must be your cock not hard. One must be your cock hard. One must be the area between your cock and balls (taint). One must be your asshole. One must be your face. Other than those 5 specific pictures, the rest can be whatever you like as long as they show off "you".

I want quality results. Remember, details are important!

As per instructions, confirm receipt of this task and ask any questions you may have at that time.

Mistress BF

Task 2

10 things you would consider punishments... Perhaps ones you think of as traditional punishments... Or just things you hate to do in your daily life. (Remember I'll punish you how I like and I might punish you if you send me pansy punishments.)

10 things you would like to earn as rewards. Choose wisely! (Again, that doesn't mean I'm going to give these out as rewards.)

You have 24 hours.

Mistress BF

Task 3

10 things you like about yourself (physically or mentally)

10 things you dislike about yourself (physically or mentally)

10 things you like in others (physically or mentally)

10 things you dislike in others (physically or mentally)

Due in 48 hours.

Mistress BF

Washing Master

I'll turn on the water and get it to the temperature I like... which is super hot. Then I'll get in first so I can be warm. You get in after me and stand under the water for a few minutes. Hotels always have bar soap... which is what I prefer anyway. You stand mostly out of the water and I'll stand under it. That way I can control when you get water on you and when you don't. I use my hands to lather the soap so I can feel your body. I don't want the washcloth in the way.

You have your back to me and I start with your neck, rubbing the soap on you and lathering it as I go with both hands. I wash your back and move my hands around your body and wash your chest.... back up around your shoulders....down your arms. All while I'm pushing my breasts against your back. Then down your stomach with my arms wrapped around you... down to your cock and wash it quickly. My hands are just on your cock... no balls... then back to your butt... and your asshole. I push my slippery finger in a little and back out. Then I move and push you under the shower, facing out.

I get on my knees and start at the bottom... washing your feet, knees, thighs. I wrap my hands around you to reach your butt and wash it again. Then between your legs washing from the back to the front... this time I linger and wash your balls and cock more thoroughly. Your cock is hard.

I put down the soap and run my hands over you to rinse you. I touch your cock all over... playing with your balls...massaging them as they become less and less slippery as the soap washes away. I'm in no hurry. I just want to touch you. I open my mouth and it's all wet from the water. I take in the head of your cock and start sucking you.

The water is running down your chest... on my face and head. I can't look up at you because the water is in my face and all over you. My eyes are closed. I make my hand soapy again and massage your balls and your ass, sliding my fingers in whenever I feel like it. I taste your cum and move... grabbing your hand and putting it on your cock so you can finish yourself.

You spray cum all over my face, my neck, down my chest and wipe your cock off on my lips. I love the feeling of power I have bringing you the ultimate pleasure. I love being between your legs.

Yo – Yo

fat ~ skinny
skinny ~ fat

long hair ~ short hair
short hair ~ long hair

new ~ old
old ~ new

make it hurt
do it softly

stop
go

wait
ok

hide behind appearances
be exposed

beauty
geek

push me away
pull me back

Yesterday I hated you ~
today I love you...

Blowjob for Master

I'll put you in a bed in this scenario. I'll make you lie face-down. You're naked. I'm naked. Since you're on your stomach, you can't do much. So I climb on top and straddle your waist, then slide my pussy down across your butt so I'm full on you and I rub on you like a cat. I'm rubbing my breasts on your back and my pussy on your butt. That part is for me because I'm horny and I need some relief.

Then I suck your ear lobe and kiss down your neck... sinking my teeth into that tender meat where your neck meets your shoulder.... running my teeth and nails down your back. I bite the top of your ass. I'm being so mean.

I'll be nice and kiss where your ass meets your leg... and keep kissing until I get between your legs. Then lick your balls and that tender spot between them and your asshole... and push on it with my tongue.

You are wiggling to turn over so I let you... and start rubbing my whole body all over you again... and yes that's also for me. I take your cock and rub it on my pussy and get it all wet.

You think we are going to fuck and you try to push yourself into me... but I move off and slide down you. I push your legs apart and make room for me to sit. I kiss your thighs and suck them... hard. Kissing you and nuzzling around and around, not touching your cock.

I look at you and you look at me. I know you want me to hurry the fuck up already. But, the teasing is so fun. You have an evil look in your eye, which I like. So I keep teasing... but this time I lick the head of your cock with its little slit and then move away again. And then I kiss your balls and up your cock to the head and open my mouth like an O and let just your head slide in.... and swirl my tongue around in circles... not going down your cock... just on the head. I grasp your cock with my hand and gently move it up and down. I open my mouth more.

You taste like my pussy. I'm licking the head of your cock at the same time I'm moving up and down with my whole mouth. I start applying more pressure with my hand... twisting it.

The tongue licking... the warm mouth... the twisting... is all happening at once. I'm touching your stomach... your legs... your thighs... your knees... your balls... myself... with my other hand. Steady rhythm faster and faster.

I taste your salt. I slow down. You whine. So I start again... building you back up. This time I let your cum pour into my mouth... and swallow it before you yank me up next to you. You kiss me and say, "Good girl".

Gum

Hard ~ soft ~ hard.
Always the same cycle.
Vibrant pink fades to dull blush.
Bursting with flavor to bland and tasteless.
Tongue pushing and stretching.
Lungs forcing moist air inside.
Sticky, chewy, rubbery.
Hard ~ soft ~ hard.

How I Think About Master Fucking Me

We'll meet in a hotel. I'll wear an indoor collar and you'll use it to tie me to the bed so I can't move. You'll kiss me and suck my lip into your mouth and tongue it, while touching my body. Probably I'll wear a tight dress with no panties. And you'll wear a light weight dress shirt and pants (commando). You flip me over and pull me up on all fours and make me stay like that for what seems like forever while you are just watching and staring at me. Tethered to the bed post by my neck, you make me watch you undress. Then you crawl underneath me and lie flat on your back and rip the top of my dress down exposing my breasts. You lick them like a cat and suckle the nipples. I try to move my body down closer but you push me back up. And then you put those damn nipple clamps on them. You move in front of my face and rub your cock on my cheek and tell me to open my mouth.

You push your cock in and tell me to suck it...I proceed. You say "look at me". Sucking cock makes me so fucking hot... so I start to whimper. I want relief... but you make me suck it a long, long time without letting me do anything to myself or without you touching me. But you are touching my face and wrapping your fingers in my hair and yanking on it. Suddenly you move behind me and I breathe a sigh of relief... but you just gently rub the head of your cock on my pussy lips... so gently I can barely tell you're there. I push backwards and you move away. You tell me to say what I want... I hate you... but I love you... you say look at me... and I look at you and say, "Please....fuck me....please". I am in agony.

You rub your cock on me a little harder and this time when I push back you let your cock slip inside. You reach around and take off the nipple clamps and rub my boobs hard and pinch my nipples. Then you move your hands down and while you fuck me you rub my clit. Now you have one hand on my clit... and with the other hand you shove your thumb in my pussy to get it all wet and then push it in my asshole and wiggle it. I moan and cum on your cock. You pull your cock out and tell me to look at you... while you cum all over my pussy and asshole. I feel the wet warmth caressing my folds and want you all over again in an instant.

Empty Stomach

I want more and more and more
in a magic vial,
swirling and filling and expanding.

Nothing distracts.
Nothing completes.
Always a void.

It's an ache that doesn't stop.
Tossing everything in the hole.

You think you can help.
You think the feeling will pass.
You say give it time.

How would you know when this
hasn't happened to you?

Oh...wait for a moment...
I forgot!
I'm full!
I'm satisfied!
I'm happy!

Then there's a trigger.
It's small.
I try to not think.
I try to stay busy.

It's small, but too big to ignore.

The hunger, the ache
is back.

A Strap-On/Spank-Filled Fantasy
(Y is capitalized to show respect to the Master in the scenario.)

I imagined it was You sitting in a chair with your back to a large window, which framed you like a picture. You were holding Lauren on Your lap. She was looking into Your eyes and You were stroking her breasts which were thrust/smashed onto Your chest. Your cock was hard against her stomach and seeping cum.

I was standing behind her grasping her hips and thrusting my strap-on into her pussy... very, very slowly. I was looking at Your face instead of at her. She was moaning and pushing back against me. With each thrust into her, I could feel the pressure building against my mound. I reached around and teased her clit with my fingers, pinching it between them. And then moved my hand up to Your balls weighing them in my hand... up farther still to Your cock. I could not stroke it properly the way it was under Lauren. But You were holding her for me and didn't mind. I felt the cum and smeared it around your cock and onto her stomach. I stood back up and smacked her ass, smacked it hard, looking in wonder between the red marks I had left on her and Your face. I felt nervous to have You watching my face as I got so turned on and my face was red.

I was being too slow and gentle. You instructed me to fuck her harder because she needed it. You leaned over and bit and suckled on the side of her neck, and that pissed me off enough that I did fuck her hard, pulling my fake cock all the way out and then slamming it balls-deep into her dripping snatch. She was moaning louder and louder and I went back to my attentions on her clit. She was in a delirious state. Running my hands all over her body, moving my thrusting hips in circles, I knew I must make her cum before I could, but I wanted so badly to reach under the strap-on to find my clit.

I could feel cum leaking down my inner thigh. All my attentions I put on making her cum. She finally broke in Your arms and collapsed onto You. I reached under the strap on, but You stopped me. You pushed her off of you and onto the floor in a heap and dragged me over in front of the window by my hair. I could see people walking by on the street below. The window was open. You pushed me over so my hands were on the window sill and my ass was in the air exposed to You. I felt You slide into my gushing hole. You proceeded to fuck me as hard as I had fucked Lauren. I was attempting to quiet my groans of pleasure, because of the strangers below.

You pulled out of me suddenly and whispered in my ear, "If you do not like this enough to express it, then I guess a punishment is in order." I was afraid my punishment was the truncation of this sexual encounter, but You clearly had other ideas. I fell against the window and had to prevent myself from falling through it when I felt Your hard smack on my bare ass. I picked myself back up and got into position and held it as You spanked my bottom over and over. It was evenly red and stinging all over both cheeks when Your hand landed on my pussy and You started spanking my pussy and clit. It hurt and I squirmed to get away and started begging You to stop.

You grabbed my ass and sank Yourself back into me. This time I didn't hesitate to moan and scream and beg you to keep going. I wanted to touch myself so badly, but all I could do was grip the sill so I wasn't pushed out to plummet several floors to my death. Mercifully, You reached around my hips and spanked my clit. The rhythm was slow and steady and I felt the pressure building. I stopped breathing and groaned while you bent over, bit my back, and Your cream mixed with mine. I was so grateful to be granted the release. My legs were like jelly and I collapsed in a heap on the floor, like Lauren.

Get Out of My Head

Drill a hole.
Blow in my ear.
Tilt my head.
Guilt goo oozes out.

Slice open the top.
Unhinge my skull.
Don rubber gloves.
Fish the anxiety
out of my brain.

Rip my hair out.
Pull the doubt
along with the roots.

Chop off my ear.
Hook your finger
around the hate
and drag it out.

Behead me.
Pick out the anger,
mistrust, despair, boredom.
Inject me with hope.

Sew me back up
and I'll try again.

A Playdate Provided by Master

Master takes us to a club so we can have a little "date". But he's more like our chaperone or bodyguard. Far across the room he sits, sipping a drink, just to make sure we are safe. We both wear miniskirts and tight hot tops. They are jean skirts. The club is playing a fast upbeat hip hop song, so we get into the music, dancing, laughing, showing off for each other and the guys (including Master) watching us. We touch hands. We grind on each other. We dirty dance.

We are hot and thirsty, so we head to the bar holding hands. Several guys ask if they can buy us drinks. We say sure, that way we don't have to buy them. We talk to them a little bit, but for the most part ignore them (ha-ha). We head back to the dance floor. The DJ switches it up and starts to play a slow set of songs. We don't care. We want to dance. So we start slow dancing with each other. The rubbing and guys watching us starts to turn us on. We begin kissing and caressing there in front of everyone. I whisper in your ear that I'm getting really turned on, and bite your neck. You moan a little louder than you should. I decide we need relief.

We walk hand in hand to the restroom, go in a stall together, and lock the door. The bathroom is plush inside in shades of pink and black. We kiss roughly, our hands in each other's hair and cupping asses. We have hidden mini vibrators in our jean skirts and we get them out, turn them on, and push them onto our clits, using our free hands to touch each other, our tits, our skin, and our hands. We are still kissing and moaning. The buzzing vibrators and our own moans fill the room and close our ears to the pulse of the dance floor. You cum first, and make a low groan against my mouth. That makes me cum. We open our eyes, look at each other, and giggle.

After we clean up, and re-hide our secret vibes, we leave the bathroom, heading back to the dance floor. Master catches our eyes and winks, because he knows what we were up to in the club restroom.

Tree Energy

My skin's on fire.
Your body heat melts me
from the inside out.

Your dripping beads of sweat
nourish my body.
I want to
grow tall like you.

I need to be on you,
and in you,
and around you.

Thinking... how can I climb you?
Help me.
Take me higher and farther.

When my body slides up yours,
I feel tremors inside...
tiny earthquakes of energy.
Are they coming from me or you?
I have no clue.

But, I can't stop until
energy is released.
The friction is igniting our energy.
I fear for our safety.
This is turning into a forest fire.

The Mistress of the House and Her Slave

She was glad to be born white, one of the privileged. Her life was one of ease: chamber maids and parlor maids, housekeepers and butlers and, yes, slaves, for this is the Deep South, the heart of slavery. She had just returned from a debutante luncheon, soon to begin preparations for a ball to be held for one of her young cousins. The day was balmy and humid with late summer heat. Her husband had been driven into the city on affairs of government. She rang for the maid, who brought her fresh lemonade from which the pulp had been carefully strained.

She sat on the verandah. She savored the cold tartness of the lemonade. She enjoyed so much the sight of the sunlit fields of cotton, with their broad sweep and green richness. And she enjoyed, too, the sight of the big, strong slaves at their labor. Incredible how much they accomplished in so a short time! They were all black, of course, - as black as she was porcelain white. Their skin, flexing and bulging as the sheathed muscles worked their strength upon the tasks at hand, intrigued her with its difference from her own. She wanted to draw closer to them… just to watch. But such interest would be considered improper for a lady. So, assuring herself that she was free from the attentions of the house servants, she glided unseen down the tree line in her full yellow dress.

She found a spot in dappled sunlight under a white ash, the foliage of which shielded her from sight, yet left her own view unhindered. As she gazed she leaned against the tree. From behind her there was a noise. Startled, she turned to see him. The one she had always watched the most. Smooth black skin, shirtless, sweat dripping from his chest. She stared at him. They stared at each other for a long, long time.

He moved closer; and she did not move away. He must have taken that as a cue for he moved even closer, reached out his huge hand, and touched her. He snaked it up the back of her neck under her hair and pulled her head back, exposing her throat. He leaned down and bit her jugular. Not hard, but enough. The smell of his unwashed body stung her. She moaned and tried to twist from his grasp. He used the leverage on her head to twist her around face first toward the huge tree. Off balance, she reached out for the tree. He took the opportunity to pull down the front of his breeches. She felt his dirty hands on the back of her dress. He was lifting it up. Too late she realized his intent. His size and strength were far above her. And, he pushed himself inside her, pinning her against the tree. "God, no! He'll tear me!" She was going to be ripped apart. He was so much bigger than she was used to. She started crying.

He stopped, moved her hair aside, and started biting and sucking on her neck. That started a fire straight down to where he had her pinned. She flooded his hardness all the way to the base. He felt it and slammed his hips upward, pulling out and slamming back into her over and over. Each thrust forced from her a harsh grunt. Each thrust bucked her hard against the rough bark of the tree. She tightened her grip and waited for the pounding to stop. He finally groaned deep like an animal and pulled out fast splashing his finish all over her inner thighs. Her dress fell to the ground when he let go and he pulled his pants back up. She kept her head down and trembled. But he wanted more. With his callused hand, he grabbed her chin and held her so she was forced to look at his face… the face of the slave who just took her by force. He leaned forward and finally put his lips to hers. She moaned and parted her lips. His tongue conquered her mouth.

When he walked back to the fields she had no doubt to whom she belonged.

It's Beauty

The leaves are thin like tissue paper,
their color pale like cantaloupe flesh.
I traveled far to make myself a
second skin to cover my bones.
Now I search for shrooms to stuff under the leaves.
I'm a delicate scarecrow inside.
It's true.

Pressure: A Dream

We were at the animal feed store. I used to always go there with my dad growing up. I'd talk to the check out guys inside and then walk through the mill part and out the back and down the stairs to get back in the truck after they'd loaded the feed. In my dream, however, the back stairs leading down to our truck were a lot higher and longer. So, anyway... you were kind of my dominant (Master) in the dream. I followed you in to order our feed and I was talking to the guys up front. We walked through the sweet smell of molasses to the back and at the top of the stairs you grabbed me roughly and said, "Did you like flirting with those guys in there?" I just winced because I knew I was in trouble for doing a bad thing and had maybe done it on purpose to push your buttons. So, you reached around and grabbed my crotch. I had jeans on. You pulled me back against the front of you and were squeezing and rubbing my crotch through my jeans. I started walking forward to get away from you and down the stairs and to the truck. There were guys milling about loading feed. I was bent over to try to change the feeling, but it felt too good. Usually in a Master/sub relationship the sub is not allowed to orgasm unless the Master says so. What you were doing felt really good and I knew I was going to. That's why I was trying to wiggle away from you. You knew it too and kept rubbing me bent over behind me. We were almost to the bottom of the stairs and I was almost home free when I grabbed the railing and came from the pressure of your hand. Then I woke up, and, was all wet between my legs.

Slippery When Oiled

My friend, who is about 20 years older than me, invited me back to his house to take a look at his extensive artwork and book collection. How could I say no to that innocent invitation?

He lives on several acres of wooded and shaded land with a pond. The house is a modernized log cabin. Not the kind made of real logs, but has the look and feel of that. It's country, cozy, and warm with a fireplace and soft plush rugs on the wooden floors. It's beautiful really, and I feel at home instantly. I'm wearing a long furry winter coat, long dress, and boots. He takes my coat and boots at the door and tells me to start looking around… feel free to wander how I like.

The artwork and books have me lost to the world around me. I go in the bathroom and see massage oil sitting on the vanity. He's told me stories of how he enjoys oiling and massaging women and I want to feel the oil on me as soon as I see the bottle. I grab it and take it out into the living room where he's reading a book by the fireplace. I hold it out to him, not saying a word. He sets down his book, picks up a big piece of fabric and lays it in front of the fireplace, then takes the bottle from me, not saying a word. I lay down on the blanket face down. He pushed my dress up around my waist. I have no underwear on as none were clean, but I'm not embarrassed. I feel him drizzling the cold oil on my butt, down my thighs and calves. I tense up from the shock of the cold. He blows on my skin to enhance it. I feel tightly coiled now and wonder if this was a bad idea.

Finally, his large warm hands land on my thighs and start working my flesh. He touches and rubs me all over avoiding the crack of my ass and between my legs. It's so relaxing I feel near falling asleep, until his fingers start moving between my legs. I think it's an accident, but when he rubs oil on my asshole, it's clearly no accident. He's pushing gently. My whole body is awake and alert again.

He tells me to roll over and take off my dress, which I do. He drizzles the oil on my chest and down my arms and stomach and repeats the relaxing motions. I'm like jelly. I couldn't move if I wanted to. Then his hands move down lower. I know it's no accident and I wonder how far he will take it.

His fingers oil my labia and up around my clit. My legs are barely spread apart. He rubs me over and over in circles all over my mound and thighs and lips and hood, massaging the whole of my body in turn as well to keep me warm and oiled.

My eyes are half-open, but I'm watching his face. I can tell by his flush he is turned on too.

I'm keeping my legs fairly close together. He keeps working me between my legs. The need to add more oil is gone, as I'm gushing. He keeps pulling the moisture up my lips and around my clit and under and over my hood. Every few minutes he slowly adds more pressure, focusing more and more on my clit. I'm breathing very shallowly. He has been rubbing me all over for over an hour and I can't take it anymore. It's difficult for me to orgasm with people, AND he's watching my face. But, I can't hold it in any longer. I WANT to cum. I stop breathing and arch my back as it hits me. He keeps his fingers and the pressure on me as my pussy pulses cum out in a river.

When I finally open my eyes and gasp for breath I hear him groan under his breath and close his eyes. He is cumming in his pants. And, I'm instantly turned on again.

I lean up and kiss him on the mouth. I'm glad I came to visit him and look forward to the next slippery episode…

Nylon, Pink Ball Gag, and Peach Pie: A Photo Shoot Gone Wild

This particular photographer was a friend known for his unique style of bondage and fetish photography, so I knew it would be an interesting shoot when I signed up for it.

It would take place at his house, in the basement studio where he shot the bulk of his work. When I arrived he was preparing a peach pie. The kitchen already smelt of sugary goodness. He told me to have a seat while he finished up. As I turned to locate a chair, he said, "Oh wait, we might as well do this now", and grabbed my wrists together. I could feel him tying them tightly together with nylon. When he was done and moved back, I sat down.

He walked over to the counter and grabbed a slice of peach. It was dripping down his fingers and the side of his hand. He pushed it between my lips. I ate the entire slice from his fingers, then licked and suckled between his fingers and the pads of his fingers, nipping them with my teeth. His face was close to mine watching me. When his fingers were licked clean and I was licking my lips he bent over and kissed me, pushing harshly with his tongue into my mouth to open it. I moaned and tried to get up to get closer to him. He abruptly broke the kiss and moved away reaching for something behind me. He pulled out a bubble gum pink ball gag and proceeded to fit it to my mouth and strap it on me. I severely disliked it. I couldn't talk, and breathing through my nose was making me start to drool a little bit.

He pulled me up and bent me over the table. I could hear him rustling around behind me. I realized he had gotten his camera after I heard the shutter releasing. He was shooting me bent over and splayed out on his kitchen table with my mouth gagged and my wrists bound.

My skirt was pushed up and my underwear yanked down around my knees…more shooting. Despite my discomfort in the situation I was starting to feel myself leaking down my inner thighs.

He leaned over behind me and whispered, "You are a bad girl to get yourself into this situation, aren't you?" All I could do was nod. "Bad girls need to be taught a lesson, don't they?" Nod.

He started to spank me. I thought he would just spank me a couple of times and be done, but he was spanking me over and over, all over my ass. He would spank, then caress. Sometimes his fingers would connect with my pussy as he spanked and the next slap would leave my juices spread across my ass. Five full minutes he spanked me, evenly all over. I was whimpering, crying a little, and starting to wiggle away.

He growled at me to lie still, and I did. He took a few more shots. Then, I could hear his zipper unzipping. I thought he intended to touch himself while he shot me. But, he clearly had other plans. I felt the heat of him and the pressure of thighs behind me and then he shoved his cock straight inside of me in one push. I started bucking and trying to get away. He held me down and fucked me over and over. I was incredibly turned on, but not on birth control. I was making the entire front of him a wet and sloppy mess.

Just like his previous abruptness, he roughly pulled out of me. He grabbed a perfectly cooled peach pie from the counter in front of me and pushed his cock into the beautiful lattice work. He was grinding himself into the pie and ejaculated emptying his balls into the pie while I watched.

All I could do was lie there whimpering, whining, and wishing I was a peach pie.

Katie Tries for the Big – O

22:27 Katie

i have a hard time masturbating

22:28 Carrie

you have a hard time masturbating?

it's not hard!

you need a pocket rocket

I'll mail you one?

LOL

22:29 Katie

lol

well i can't seem to get in the mood

ok are you ready for this

are you sitting down

22:29 Carrie

yep

22:29 Katie

i have NEVER had an O

22:30 Carrie

shut the fuck up

22:30 Katie

i have been having sex since i was 15 and never

nope

22:30 Carrie

holy fucking shit

22:30 Katie

i know

22:30 Carrie

like holy shit

22:30 Katie

and my ex was the best ever so if it was going to happen it would have happened then but NOPE

so i bought toys

22:31 Carrie

right

22:31 Katie

and i have been trying since my boyfriend has been gone

still no go

lol

22:31 Carrie

ok now... don't be putting the toys in you like a penis... you have to put them on the clit... you know exactly where that is??

22:32 Katie

haha well i bought this one thing that has a bullet

and oh yes

if it is going to do it that will

i have found my spot but just not there yet

i think i try too hard

haha

22:33 Carrie

LOL

I have LOTS of toys.

I have an O like every day.

 Just me.

22:33 Katie

that must be why you are always smiling lol

22:34 Carrie

you smile a lot too... How long have you held it on your clit while it was vibrating?

22:34 Katie

welllll i get to a point and i can't handle it

22:34 Carrie

maybe it's like riding a bike... once you get it you know how... but you have to learn first.

OKKKKK that's when you can't stop

that means you are going to cum

push through the weirdness

22:35 Katie

I KNOW and i can't handle it

you make me want to try now lol

22:35 Carrie

Because it's weird? Because it hurts?

why can't you handle it

I want to come over there and show you myself right now! lol

22:36 Katie

well it doesn't hurt it just is so intense

HAHAHAHAH

22:36 Carrie

right... that's good... you are doing it right

it will make you have to close your eyes

ok so you are not putting anything inside... right? only putting something on the clit, right?

22:39 Katie

well what i do is i use it like it is and then when i finally get myself in the mood then yes i just use the bullet on the outside

i have this spot on the top like where the hole is

22:41 Carrie

when you get wet... then kind of use your fingers and rub your wetness on your clit... for some reason that makes it easier to cum.. and hold the thing with one hand and pull back the hood of your clit gently with the other so it's completely exposed to the vibrator. Understand?

22:41 Katie

understand

this all sounds amazing that if this happens for me i might never get another job

lol

22:42 Carrie

you will not be depressed anymore if you can have an O... that will cheer you right up

22:42 Katie

and one thing i have a hard time using my fingers for things that is what i think is weird

22:43 Carrie

because you have retard fingers or you are embarrassed to put your fingers in it

hehe

22:44 Katie

haha i guess more the embar thing

well this is what i do

22:45 Carrie

now listen

22:45 Katie

cause i can never make myself wet

22:46 Carrie

you need to look at your stuff in the mirror

touch it all over

it's ok to touch it

22:47 Katie

i go and shower and then i go and put a movie in... i like girl on girl for some reason?!?!?!? and then i usually have to use lube of some type which i am out now and then i try to excite myself

i will need to check it out and look at this thing

i have NEVER looked at it

22:47 Carrie

holy fuckballs Katie! I want to smack you

go now

take me with you

22:48 Katie

haha

well.......

um ok sure

22:48 Carrie

ok now take off your pants and underwear

22:48 Katie

omg

ok

i need a different mirror

one sec

22:49 Carrie

we are going to do this shit... and the good thing is there's no pressure... if you don't have one... you just try again sometime... it's all about having fun

22:50 Katie

ok carrie ... i now have a huge mirror out

22:51 Carrie

ok good

now take off clothes

get a blanket if cold

22:51 Katie

ok

22:51 Carrie

get your bullet part too

no lube you don't need it

22:51 Katie

ok

22:51 Carrie

I will help

22:52 Katie

got it

lol

22:52 Carrie

put the mirror between your legs so you can see what you are doing

your fingers are gonna get messy so you might have to wipe the keyboard after this lol

22:52 Katie

i have a huge one propped against the couch i am on the floor

oh jesus

22:53 Carrie

good ok now just look at it for a few minutes

don't touch

look at the lips

the inner and outer

the slit

clit

hood

hole

between vag and asshole

asshole

see the colors

see the texture

see how it all connects together

now use your fingers

it's ok

and not the vibe

just fingers

22:54 Katie

ok sec

ok

i am with you now

i got behind

22:55 Carrie

ok np

now you can touch

just trace EVERYTHING

don't try to arouse... just look and touch

wiggle stuff

move it around

play with the lips

look under the hood of the clit

look at your asshole

look inside your pussy

hope I can use that word

anyway

22:57 Katie

lol yes

22:57 Carrie

use your fingers and spread it open and look in it

pink

22:57 Katie

yeah

22:58 Carrie

it's beautiful, right?

22:58 Katie

well

22:58 Carrie

we all look different

I always thought my lips were big, but the dr said nope.

So it's normal

22:58 Katie

mine look big

22:59 Carrie

yeah I wanted mine cut off

lol

ok now don't worry about me and responding if you can't

just use both hands

rub around your pussy with one

just touch all around

no rules

just whatever feels good

23:00 Katie

i feel weird using my fingers

23:00 Carrie

rub a little inside the pussy too to see if it's getting wet

I know you do... but it's so normal. We all do it.

if it's getting wet.. use your fingers to pull some of the wetness up to the clit area

23:01 Katie

ok

23:02 Carrie

is it wet? if not it's ok

23:02 Katie

a little

23:02 Carrie

ok if not a lot... put your fingers in your mouth and then back down there

23:02 Katie

ok

23:03 Carrie

it's ok to taste yourself

then you know what guys taste

so you can go back and forth between your pussy and your mouth to get it wetter if you need to

23:03 Katie

ok

23:04 Carrie

now keep touching, rubbing playing and it will get more and more wet

with the one hand not on/in the pussy

I would say use your hand you write with to touch your clit.

I use my middle finger, but some use the index.

the finger has to be wet

from mouth or pussy juice is better

you are going to rub up around under the hood area

so one hand is touching and just feeling around pussy... just experimenting what feels good

the other (writing hand) is touching clit

the finger touching the clit...

you need to rub with slight pressure

up and down the side of the clit

one side of the clit

over and over

then switch to the other side of the clit

over and over

keep this finger wet

keep going down to the pussy or finger in mouth to keep it wet

if you keep doing this over and over you will cum... since you are new this may still be too hard at first... so once everything is wet

then you could use the vibe

and use it instead of the finger

up and down side of clit

with pressure

light at first... more and more pressure as you can handle it

23:11 Carrie

I like to watch porn... so you could put that on... you said girl on girl which is good... or you can maybe mentally imagine a girl licking you and her tongue on your clit instead of your finger

everything that your fingers are doing... imagine it's her mouth

tongue under the hood... licking in all the folds and sucking the lips

pushing her tongue inside your pussy

just like your fingers

ok now close your eyes... you know what to do... relax and keep going... I will be here when you are done or decide to stop

no pressure

23:19 Katie

sooo sensitive

23:20 Carrie

I know. It's ok. Like I said there is no pressure to keep going. If you don't like it now... just try again tomorrow.

At least now you know what to do.

23:27 Katie

ok allow me to explain

i now know how to do this without using lube

i clearly did not need that

i am pretty sure i did not have one... but i was very, very close and lost it (i think)... and after that i was really sensitive, but then was not able to get that back again

i know i did not have one but man i am sure i was really close

i feel closer to myself and well you too lol

23:29 Carrie

good

yes it's hard in the beginning, but you WILL get there... this should give you something to do on your time off

lol

23:30 Katie

haha

23:30 Carrie

and that happens to me even now that I know how to do it where you will get close and then lose it

all normal

you are normal

so you are happy?

23:31 Katie

maybe i will make myself a nice dinner and woo myself

23:31 Carrie

ok I am going to bed soon... keep me posted...

23:31 Katie

yeah i am happy

23:31 Carrie

and I'm happy to answer questions anytime

23:31 Katie

haha well thank you

we have bonded

23:32 Carrie

talk soon babe

Orgasm

Waves in a lake... lead to mindless pressure and tingling... hard to breath... sometimes not breathing at all... barely moving....until I break. It feels like breaking, shattering, energy exploding outward. My head snaps back and I arch my back and cry out/whimper at the same time. It lasts for a minute to 90 seconds... pulsing in my pussy... similar to how a guy pushes cum out. I actually have before. Then I open my eyes and can breath/swallow again.

Change is Good?

Meeting happens purely by chance.
I hadn't been looking and searching for someone.
Or maybe I had?

You gave me a reason to think of possibilities.
We had a mental adventure upon our first discussion.
And, we've traveled the recess of our brains together ever since.

Your thoughts and ideas now mingle with my own.
Who came first? Your idea or mine?

You've changed me. I've changed you.
We've changed. Together.

I wish I was a butterfly...

.....in your backyard....
wearing my string bikini and flitting over the grass in my bare feet. Twirling and dancing to the music. My head is back and the breeze blows my hair around. I clutch fistfuls of uncapped body markers. It's approaching twilight, but the day is still rich with a soft golden light.

Your swim shorts hang low on your hips as you stalk me... waiting your chance to grab me and slow me down. Make me stop and play with you.

I twirl and move closer and farther away, teasing you, enticing you to try. Each time you can't resist and reach for me. I slash at you with the markers in my hands and put more and more colorful streaks all over your body. Sometimes you catch me for a second until I wiggle away, leaving behind just the brightly colored markings that I was there.

Ooooh, too close! You have my hair wrapped around your hand! You grab markers out of my hand, kiss me and, holding my mouth against you, drag the markers all over, leaving your imprint on me. I melt against you and kiss your lips, sucking their fullness into mine. Then I remember... I want to be free!... and struggle away from you.

I see the outline of your cock in your shorts and reach into my bikini to touch myself while keeping a safe distance. Intensely you watch me for the next opportunity when I will get too close or just close enough. You are not moving so I move closer to you and run one marker from the top of your throat down your chest, down your stomach, down your shorts. I draw on your cock while it's still covered... up and down.

I'm watching your face. Your jaw is twitching. I don't see it coming. You have me flipped around, yank down my bikinis and shove your cock inside my pussy from behind. I groan and drop all the markers to put my hands on the ground.

I'm trying to be quiet, but I think the neighbors can hear. My pussy starts leaking down your balls. Harder. Harder. Harder. I reach for a marker and trail it up the inside of your thigh and even mark the inside of my own thighs.

I stand up and am still on your cock facing away from you. I wrap my arms around your neck and you bite my neck and move your hands up to pinch my nipples, tracing the sides of my breasts first. I move off your cock and hold it against my pussy, rubbing it forward and back on my tender lips, making it wetter and wetter. The inside of my thighs are even getting wet.

You take it away from me and rub my pussy juice to my ass and back. You kiss me on the mouth and then shove me forward again. I struggle to stay standing while I can feel the head of your cock pressuring my asshole. I relax and it's all the way in my ass. For a few moments you stay motionless, then start to thrust hard. I try to get away, but too late! It hurts, but my pussy likes it and leaks its hot juice down my legs. I can't be quiet anymore! I'm moaning loudly for all to hear as you go faster and faster. I can hear your groaning and gasping. You pull out of my ass and, as you do, you shoot cum all over my back, spraying it from my hair to my asshole pushing the head back against my ass, letting the last bit ooze into my hole.

I collapse on the ground. My legs are weak from holding the position. I lie on my back and regain strength to continue my butterfly dance...

About The Author

Carrie "Butterfly" Turner, is a mixed media artist who focuses on 3D collage, found object sculptures, oil pastels, repetitive designs, and vibrant colorful photographic portrait art. She strives to achieve her artistic vision through the use of found objects like bottle caps, trash, and treasures she finds on the sidewalk.

"I see the world in snapshots. Everywhere I look I see a photograph. I think that's the true sign of an artist or an artist at heart. Most people have that inside of them... it just needs to be cultivated. I am always trying to push my art to be as creative as possible."

Carrie started her art education at a young age, doing creative projects with her mother. Art was always her favorite subject in school as well. She became Art Club Secretary her Junior year in high school, then President of Art Club in her Senior year at John Glenn High School. She has taken numerous courses in art at the college level and received a Bachelor of Business Administration with a focus in marketing from Ohio University.

Since college, Carrie has gone on to develop a healthy and fruitful resume of her achievements. Carrie works under the name "Butterfly", a name she received from supporters of her art, because of her love for butterflies. "We are always growing and changing, ugly to beautiful butterflies." She has taken the metamorphosis of the butterfly to heart in creating an astounding evolution of work.

In 2008, she was chosen as one of 100 local Zanesville, Ohio artists to complete a 7-foot vase for the "Vase in Place" project in Zanesville. She designed the piece, an explosion of multi-colored circles on a black background, to be visible from a distance and bring color and pop art to the environment in which it was placed. The vases were auctioned off with proceeds going to support local art groups.

In 2010 and again in 2011, she was one of 24 artists chosen to create a recycled art sculpture at Fountain Square in Cincinnati.

Her art is featured in private galleries in Ohio, Florida, New Jersey,

Massachusetts, and Australia.

Recently, she has continued experimenting with found objects; recycling "trash" into art, 2D/3D collages, mixing traditional acrylic techniques with 3D collage, wax on canvas, item repetition to create a strong visual image, watercolor on Yupo synthetic paper, and portraiture. Her work has been described as "lots of feeling [in it], and it is a great reflection of society, waste, and beauty" and she "brings out the beauty in things people shy away from".

2011 saw the inception of "Butterfly's Art" and the acquisition of her studio space in Zanesville at Tower Studios with her long-time friend and art soul mate, Natasha Oliver. In May of 2012, she and Natasha joined forces with 3 other local artists: Allen Deaver, Joleen Kinsel, and Joe Murphy to create The Artist Collective, a studio space where the three women continue to work, share art with the public, host monthly events on First Fridays - exhibiting the art and creations of local artists as well as their own work, and offer classes to the public. She is now a full-time artist, art instructor, curator, model, art catalyst/advocate/mentor/motivator, and now author. As an active and inspirational artist she is heavily scheduled for events throughout the remainder of 2014.

This is her first book.

www.facebook.com/artbybutterfly

www.ingramcontent.com/pod-product-compliance
Lightning Source LLC
Chambersburg PA
CBHW070921180426
43192CB00038B/2146